A.E.G. BOMBER.

MINISTRY OF MUNITIONS.

Technical Department—Aircraft Production.

I.C. 607.

Kingsway,

W.C. 2.

REPORT ON

A.E.G. BOMBER.

MARCH 1918.

The Naval & Military Press Ltd

Published by
The Naval & Military Press Ltd
5 Riverside, Brambleside, Bellbrook
Industrial Estate, Uckfield, East Sussex,
TN22 1QQ England

Tel: +44 (0) 1825 749494

Fax: +44 (0) 1825 765701

www.naval-military-press.com
www.military-genealogy.com

*In reprinting in facsimile from the original, any imperfections are inevitably reproduced
and the quality may fall short of modern type and cartographic standards.*

MINISTRY OF MUNITIONS.

Technical Department—Aircraft Production.

I.C. 607.

Kingsway,

W.C. 2.

REPORT ON

A.E.G. BOMBER.

MARCH, 1918.

Report on A.E.G. Bomber, G.105.

This machine was brought down by anti-aircraft fire at Achiet-le-Grand on 23.12.17.

On a label protected by celluloid, mounted on a tube in the nacelle, is the legend—" Abnahme am (Accepted on) 10/11/17."

This machine, whilst carrying a similar power plant, is very different in construction from the Gotha type, which also embraces the Friedrichshafen Bomber reported on in I.C. 619.

Whereas the latter is generally constructed of wood, ply wood being used to a very large extent throughout, in the A.E.G. steel is almost universally employed, not only in regard to the fuselage, nacelle, subsidiary surfaces and landing gear, but also in the wings themselves.

Needless to say, acetylene welding is freely resorted to throughout the construction, which, however, appears to be far from light.

On the whole, the A.E.G. aeroplane, judged by contemporary British standards of design, is decidedly clumsy, not only in detail work, but also in appearance. The performance is poor.

The leading particulars of the machine are as follows :—

Weight empty	5258 lbs.
Total weight	7130 lbs.
Area of upper wings	395.2 sq. ft.
,, ,, lower ,,	335.2 sq. ft.
Total area of ,,	730.4 sq. ft.
Loading per square foot of wing surface	9.77 lbs. per sq. ft.
Area of ailerons, each	17.9 sq. ft.
,, ,, balance of aileron	1.8 sq. ft.
Area of tail plane ...	34.0 sq. ft.
,, ,, fin ...	11.5 sq. ft.
,, ,, rudder	20.8 sq. ft.
Balanced area of rudder ...	2.6 sq. ft.
Area of elevators ...	31.2 sq. ft.
Balanced area of elevators	3.6 sq. ft.
Horizontal area of body ...	206.4 sq. ft.
Vertical ,, ,, ,,	209.2 sq. ft.
Total weight per horse power ...	13.7 lbs. approx.
Crew—Pilot and two passengers ...	540 lbs.
Armament ...	2 guns.
Engines	2 260 H.P. Mercedes.
Petrol capacity	123 gallons=861 lbs.
Oil ,,	11 gallons=110 lbs.
Water ,,	13 gallons=130 lbs.

Other dimensions are also shown on the drawings at the end of the Report.

PERFORMANCE.

(a) CLIMB, 5,000 FT. IN 10.3 MINS.

Rate of climb at 5,000 ft.—390 ft. per min.

Climb, 9,000 ft. in 23.4 mins.

Rate of climb at 9,000 ft.—235 ft. per min.

(b) SPEED AT HEIGHTS.

Level to 5,000 ft.—90 miles per hour approximately.

At 9,000 ft.—86 ,, ,, ,, ,,

(c) LANDING SPEED.

The aeroplane is best landed at a speed between 75 and 80 miles an hour; after flattening out it sinks to the ground quickly and pulls up rapidly.

(d) CONTROL.

1. Lateral—Good.

2. Elevators—Bad, especially when landing.

NOTE.—It is stated that it is not advisable to fly this machine without a passenger in the front seat.

1

CONSTRUCTION.

Wings.

As will be seen from the scale drawings, the wings are of characteristic form. The central portion consists of a rectangular centre cell permanently attached to the fuselage. The lower wings support the engines. In this centre cell the planes are set horizontally. At each side of it the lower main planes are swept upwards with a vertical dihedral of 2.75°, the top planes being kept flat, and both main planes are swept backwards in the horizontal plane to an angle of 4° for the bottom plane and 3° for the top plane. As the central portion of the upper main plane has 4 inches of negative stagger relative to the bottom plane, this difference in angle brings their tips practically vertically over one another. The angle of incidence attains a maximum of 4° at the base of the engine struts, i.e., 7 ft. 10⅜ inches from the centre. At the second strut the angle is 3½° and at the end strut 2¼°. These angles are painted in circles on the surface of the planes, evidently for the convenience of riggers. The camber of both planes is washed out gradually towards the tips, and a representative section of the main planes taken at the junction of the engine bearer struts is given in Fig. 1. For

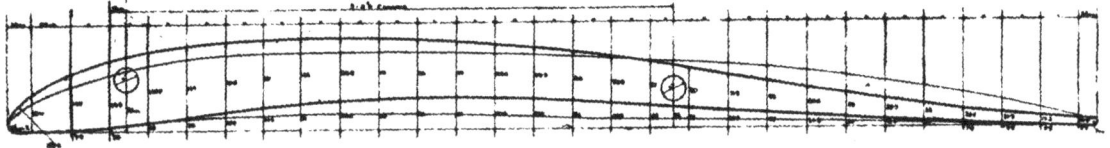

AEROFOIL SECTION A.E.G. AEROPLANE

Fig. 1.

purposes of reference the R.A.F.14 section is superimposed. This figure also shows the position of the main spars, which are of steel tube. These are 50 mms. in outside diameter, but their wall thickness is not at present known. In order to allow the thinning down of the wing section, these tubes are flattened out towards the extremity of the wing. They are chamfered down to a narrow end and a flat plate acetylene welded on to each side; thus at the spar tip the section is roughly rectangular. The main spars are kept parallel throughout the whole of their length and are attached to the central cell by means of pin joints, similar to those on the Friedrichshafen. The ribs are of solid wood and are constructed as shown in Fig. 2. It is rather notable in

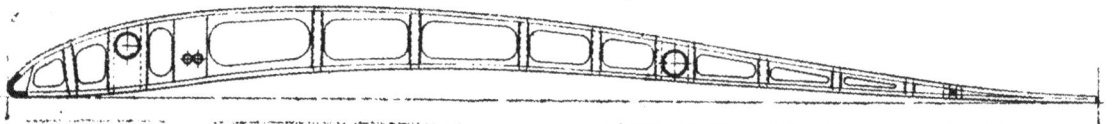

Fig. 2.

comparison with other German machines of all types that ply wood is almost entirely absent. In the A.E.G. construction the rib webs are perforated and strengthened by wooden uprights at intervals and are glued into a grooved flange. The ribs are placed 300 mms.—325 mms. apart—and are not directly or firmly attached to the spars on which they are a relatively loose fit. Passing through the ribs of the bottom plane and extending from their junction with the centre section to the extreme outside strut are two steel tubes, approximately 17 mms. in diameter, which act as housings for the aileron control wires. These tubes are very strong, and it is thought possible that they are also counted upon to lend rigidity to the wing structure. The leading edge, which is of the usual semi-circular section, acts as a distance piece, as also does the wire trailing edge. Thirteen inches in front of the last named is a stringer formed of a steel rod. Apart from this, the spars are the only longitudinal members of the wings. Between the main ribs are false ribs running from the leading edge to a point a few inches behind the leading spar and applying only to the upper surface. One of these false ribs is sketched in Fig. 3. It is secured as shown in the

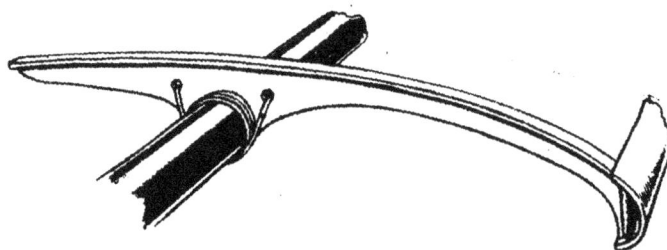

Fig. 3.

2

sketch by means of a semi-circular saddle and a wrapping of tape which passes as shown through holes in the rib. Where it meets the leading edge it is furnished with triangular packing pieces, which locate and hold it in position. The lower plane is covered as to its upper surface with sheet metal immediately under the engines, whilst between them and the fuselage is fixed a strip of corrugated aluminium which acts as a footway. The fabric is attached in the usual manner and is stitched to the ribs both top and bottom. The two surfaces are stitched together behind the metal rod, which acts as a stringer, and by this means the actual trailing edge wire is relieved of a certain amount of tension. The wing structure is internally braced by means of steel tubular cross-pieces and stranded cables. A single fitting is employed for the attachment of the interplane struts and for that of the bracing tubes. This fitting is shown in Fig. 4. It is a tight fit on the spar, to which it is fixed by a bolt, and is formed with an extension lug which acts, as shown, as an anchorage for the bracing tube, whilst a sideways extension of the same lug carries an eye for the bracing wire. It is provided with a cup-shaped upper extension, into which there is screwed a steel dome which carries the ball of the strut socket fitting and also acts as a wiring plate for the interplane bracing wires. As shown in the sketch, the fabric is run into the space between the upper and lower flanges of this fitting, the whole making a very neat job.

STRUTS.

These are of streamline section steel tube and of uniform dimensions throughout. The section is 92 mms. long by 48 mms. broad. The ends are sharply tapered down, and into them is welded a cupped ferrule which drops on to the ball shown in sketch Fig. 4 and is there held in position by a cotter pin. The attachment is shown complete in Fig. 5. This joint gives a considerable range of lateral freedom, as is the usual practice on machines of German design.

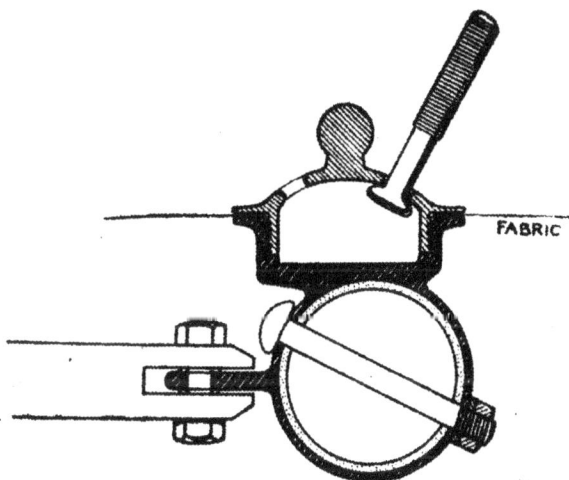

Fig. 4.

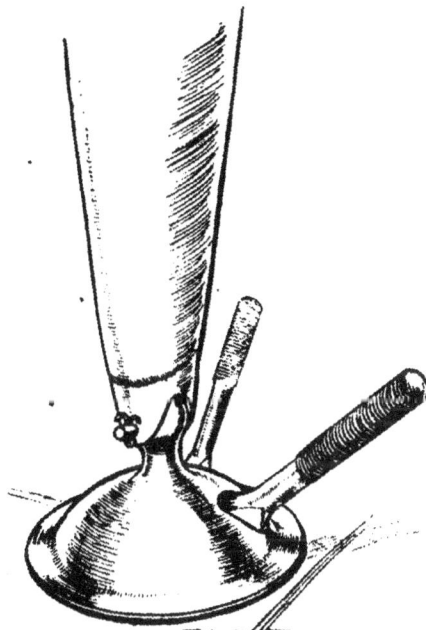

Fig. 5.

FUSELAGE.

The whole of the fuselage is built up of steel tubes welded together. It is of plain rectangular section and the cross tubes are attached directly to the main booms without the intervention of any clips. This detail of construction is shown in Fig. 6, which also illustrates the single and double lugs which are used for the purpose of securing the bracing wires. Under the nacelle and in the neighbourhood of the main petrol tanks and the bomb racks the fuselage is reinforced with thin tubular steel tie-rods. Fig. 7 shows the manner in which the upper booms of the fuselage are provided with sockets for the inclined struts of the central cell. The fitting consists of two circular steel plates welded into position to form an integral part of the frame joint, the front one of these flanges being provided with lugs for the anchorage of bracing cables. The inclined struts are secured by a ring of short set screws wired together as shown. If appearances are to be trusted, this form of attachment, whilst being strong and convenient, is excessively heavy. Unlike the practice which is pursued in the Friedrichshafen Bomber, wherein the main frame consists of three separate sections, that of the A.E.G. is in one piece from stem to stern. The longerons are 30 mms. in diameter and the transverse members 30 mms., these dimensions being retained up to the extreme tail end. The nose part of the frame is covered in with three-ply wood, but behind this a double covering of fabric is used, under which the tubular construction is completely hidden. Behind the after cockpit a single covering only is adopted and laced the whole of its length so that it is removable in its entirety.

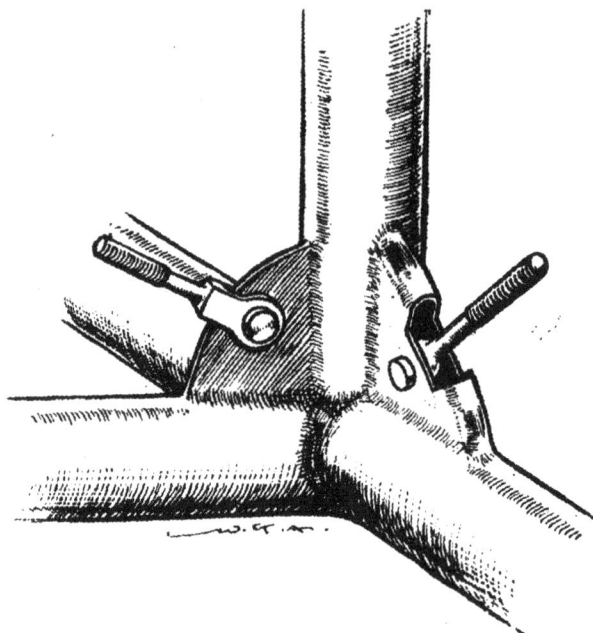

Fig. 6.

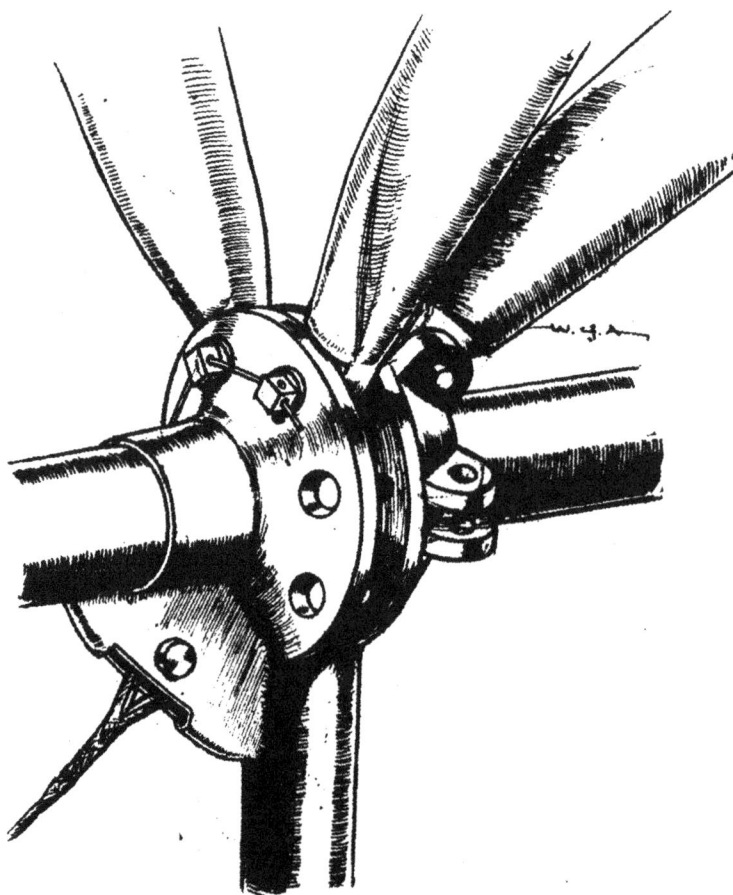

Fig. 7.

ENGINE STRUTS.

These are of streamline steel tubing and embrace joints of a somewhat similar type to those used on the interplane struts; that is to say, a certain amount of free movement is provided. The mounting of the engines is clearly shown in the front and side elevations. In front there are four struts which converge to a joint on the leading spar, whilst at the rear there are two struts which meet at a joint on the trailing spar. The attachment of the former is shown in Fig. 8. The bell-shaped housing attached to a cup on the spar joint contains a ball-ended set screw which screws into the foot of the four struts which are here united by welding. The inclined transverse struts are taken from the spars to the engine mounting and cross struts from thence again to the upper booms of the fuselage. In order to provide simplicity of erection these subsidiary struts are provided with a means of adjustment as shown in Fig. 9. At one end they terminate in a ball-ended set screw screwed into the tapered end of the strut and secured by a lock nut.

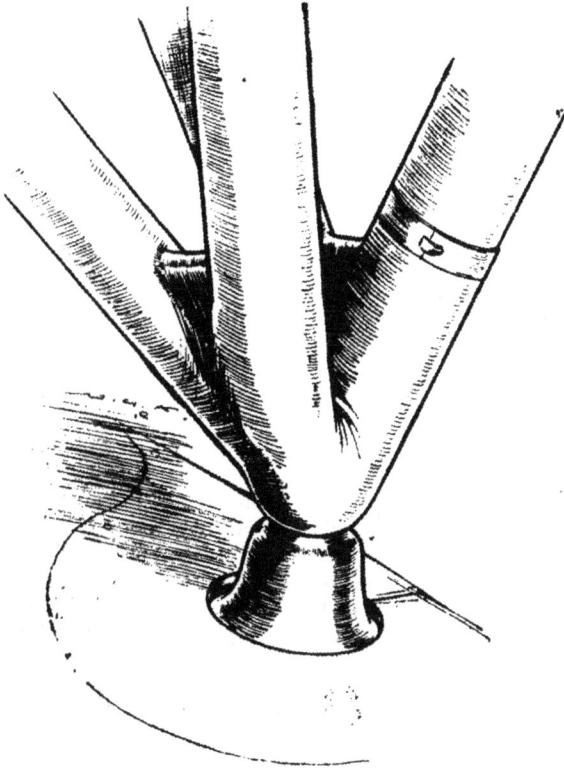

FIG. 8.

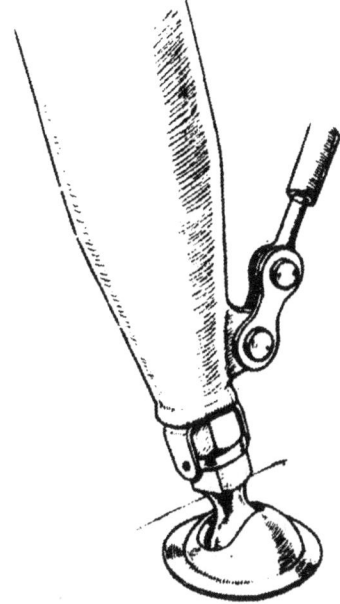

FIG. 9.

ENGINE MOUNTING.

The engine bearers are of steel rectangular section, measuring 40 mms. high by 30 mms. broad, with a wall thickness of approximately 2 mms. These bearers are welded to the struts which support them, as shown in Fig. 10, and for the greater part of their length are reinforced by a system of tubular tie-rods also welded in position. Box attachments welded to the engine bearers, as shown in Fig. 11, are provided for the crankchamber holding-down bolts. The engine is not directly mounted on the steel bearers, but upon ½ inch wooden washers. Owing to the deformation inseparable from so much welding the engine mounting is of very clumsy appearance, and, in fact, the quality of welding does not appear to be up to previous German standards, but the construction would appear to be light.

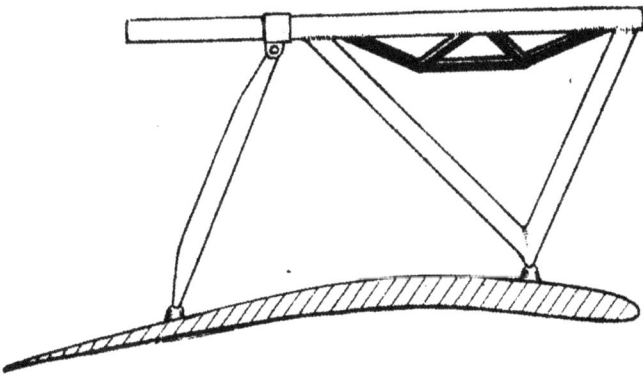

FIG. 10.

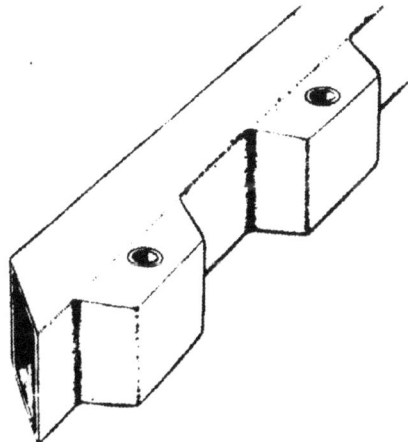

FIG. 11.

ENGINE FAIRING.

As shown in the photographs, the engines are almost completely enclosed in a fairing composed of detachable aluminium panels. The necessary framework and clips are provided for panels totally enclosing the engine, but it would seem that this bonnet right over the heads of the cylinders has been discarded. The tubular framework which supports the panels is an elaborate piece of work comprising a multiplicity of welded joints. It consists of 16 mm. tubes, to which are attached lugs for carrying the necessary turn-buttons. The framework is made in two halves so as to be easily detachable, and a joint for that purpose is made, as shown in the sketch Fig. 12. It will be noticed that a narrow slot for the exit of air passing over the engine is provided at the rear end of the engine egg, an opening of somewhat similar dimensions being between the two halves of the radiator.

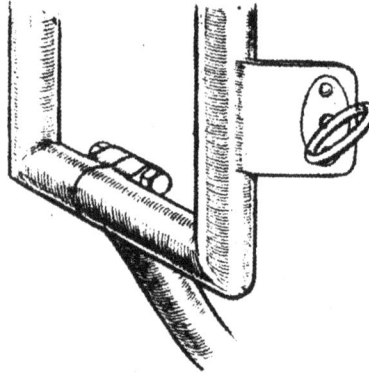

FIG. 12.

ENGINES.

The engines are the standard 6-cylinder 260 H.P. Mercedes. These engines have already been fully described, and no important novel points are adopted. A new shape has been adopted for the exhaust pipe, and this is clearly shown in one of the photographs—an inverted cone is placed in the belled mouth of the pipe. The usual water pump greaser is fitted and worked by a lever in the pilot's cockpit. It is of rather less clumsy design than that of the Friedrichshafen, but employs the same principle. The throttle is interconnected with the ignition advance as described in the Friedrichshafen report. A small fitting, the purpose of which is not very clear, is attached to the carburetter, and consists, as shown in Fig. 13 of a bell-shaped cover over the top of the float chamber, not directly connected thereto, but supported on a bracket clipped to the main water pipe. The bell is free to slide up and down the stem of the bracket, on which it is a very loose fit, but is prevented from falling over the float chamber by a small washer. It is conjectured that this fitting may have for its purpose the prevention of petrol having access to the hot exhaust pipe in the event of the machine turning over. Between the bell and the float chamber is a clearance of about ¼ inch.

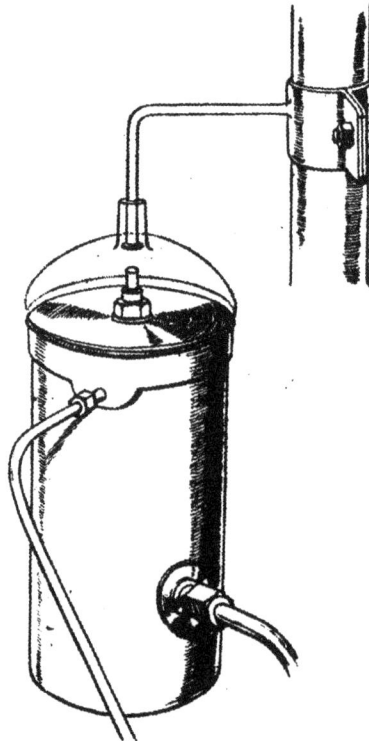

FIG. 13.

6

PETROL SYSTEM.

The petrol system employed on the A.E.G. is as set out diagrammatically in Fig. 14. There are two main tanks, each of 270 litres—95 gallons total capacity, and these are placed under the pilot's seat in the main cockpit. Two subsidiary tanks used solely for starting purposes and giving a gravity supply are mounted in the centre section of the top main plane and are of roughly streamline form. Beneath them is a small cowling containing their level gauges, which are visible from the pilot's seat. On the right hand side of the main cockpit is fitted a hand-operated wing pump, the object of which is to draw petrol from either of the main tanks and direct it to the gravity tanks. Pipes from all four tanks are taken to a distributing manifold on the dashboard, and by means of seven taps thereon the supply of petrol can be directed from any one of the tanks to either engine or both. Two additional taps are provided on the wing pump so that the fuel for the gravity supply can be drawn from either main tank as required. The photograph A clearly shows the arrangement of the petrol taps, which are of the plain plug type. It would appear that the troubles associated with this form of tap have been overcome, as they show no signs of leaking or sticking. The level of the main tanks is indicated on the dashboard by two Maximall gauges. Those attached to the gravity tanks are made by Laufer and employ the static head principle. They read up to 45 litres each, from zero to this figure being given by one and a half complete revolutions of the indicating hand.

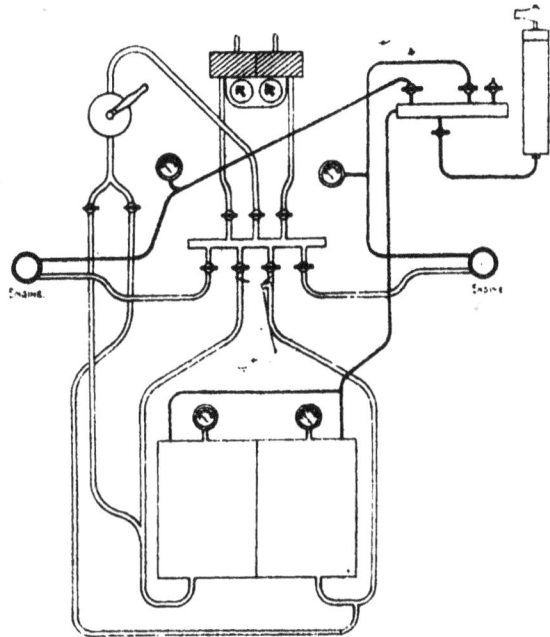

Fig. 14.

PETROL PRESSURE SYSTEM.

The sketch Fig. 14 also shows in solid lines the arrangement of the petrol pressure system. The usual pressure pump is mounted on each engine and pipes therefrom are led to a manifold mounted on the dashboard. This is also connected to a large hand pump on the right hand side of the pilot's seat. Gauges reading the pressure from each engine pump are provided, and there is also a blow-off tap for relieving the pressure of the whole system.

OIL SYSTEM.

This is the usual system as fitted to all 260 H.P. Mercedes engines. The main supply of oil is carried in the crank chamber sump and is continually being refreshed by a small additional supply of fresh oil drawn from an external tank. This tank has a capacity of 5 gallons, is of rectangular shape, and is mounted at the side of the engine nearest to the fuselage. It is provided with a visible glass level over which is a celluloid covered window let into the engine fairing, so that the oil level is visible from the pilot's seat.

RADIATOR.

Each radiator is composed of two halves bolted together, as shown in the sketch Fig. 15 which is to scale. The space between the two halves is partially covered with a sheet metal panel pierced with a hole 1' 6" high by 4" wide. The radiator is not actually honeycomb, though presenting that appearance. It consists of a series of vertical tubes with transverse gills. Each radiator cell measures 2' 3¼" high by 7½" wide, and has a uniform depth of 4". Each complete radiator is provided with two shutters of roughly streamline section. These, when fully closed, cover over about one-third of the radiating surface.

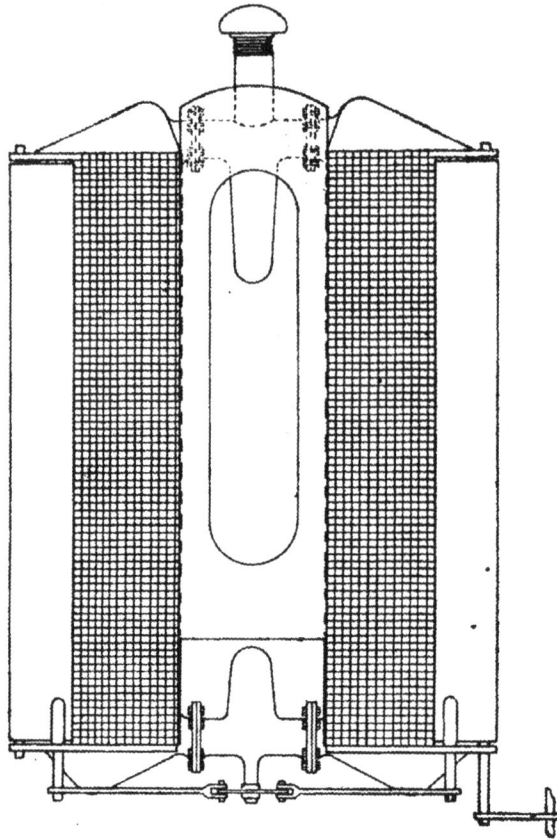

FIG. 15.

They are controlled from the pilot's seat by two levers shown in Fig. 16, which work them through universally jointed rods. The articulation in these rods is very neat and of the form shown in sketch Fig. 17. Each radiator is fitted with an electric thermometer, full details of which device have been published. The dial of this instrument is carried on the dashboard and is furnished with a switch enabling the temperature of either radiator to be independently read.

FIG. 16.

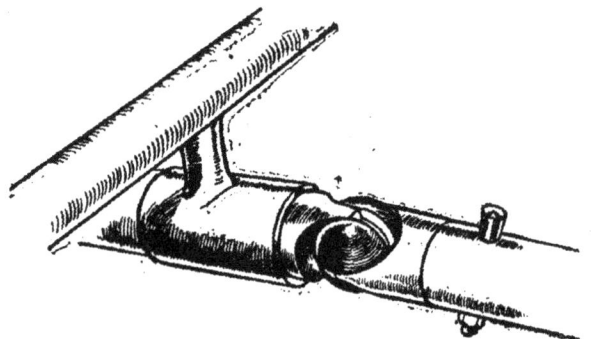

FIG. 17.

ENGINE CONTROL.

The throttle levers are of the plain twin variety, and are constructed as indicated in sketch Fig. 18. They are placed close together so as to be easily worked either in unison or separately. The connections between the levers and the carburetter are made as simple as possible, and the levers operate the throttle through a couple of universally jointed rods which extend from each side of the body to the engine eggs. The universal joints used are of the type shown in Fig. 19. there being apparently no particular desire on the part of the designer to economise weight in these details.

Fig. 18.

Fig. 19.

TAIL PLANES.

The fixed horizontal tail planes are notable for their extremely bold curvature, both top and bottom. The framework consists entirely of welded steel tubing. The leading edge of the tail plane is mounted so as to be adjustable in case of necessity, a simple bracket being used for this purpose, as illustrated in Fig. 20. This is welded on to the fuselage upright at each side and strengthened with a transverse stay. It allows the tail plane leading edge to be fixed in one of three positions. The trailing edge of the tail plane is supported each side by a streamline section steel tubular strut.

Fig. 20.

FIN.

The fin, like the fixed tail plane, has also a very strongly marked streamline section at the base tapering off to flat at the top, where it abuts against the balanced portion of the rudder. At this point its framework, which is of light steel tube, is made rigid by a couple of tubular stays bracing the rudder post to the sides of the fuselage.

RUDDER AND ELEVATORS.

These organs are built up of steel tubular framework and present no points of special interest, except that in the case of the rudder that part which is above the fixed fin is made of grooved section.

AILERONS.

As may be seen from the plan view of the complete machine, the shape of the ailerons is somewhat unusual. These are applied to the top plane only and have a chord which reaches its maximum at their extreme ends and its minimum in the centre of their length. For what purpose this peculiar shape is adopted is not clear. The framework of these ailerons is welded steel tubing, and the control crank is fitted in such a way as to lie partially hidden in a slot in the main plane. This crank is built up of welded sheet steel, and is arranged as shown in the sketch, Fig. 21, an elliptical hole being cut in the trailing edge of the main plane for the passage of the forward wire.

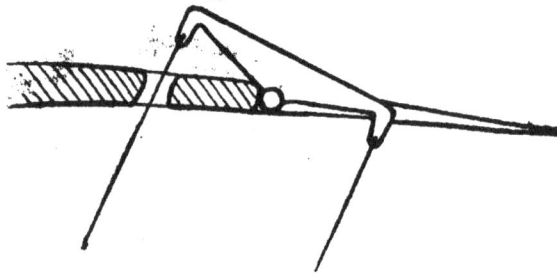

FIG. 21.

CONTROL.

The main control consists of a wheel mounted on a pivoted lever, the wheel operating the ailerons by means of a drum and cables, which pass direct over pulleys and along tubes running parallel with the wing spars and then over inclined pulleys up to the aileron cranks. The wheel column is pivoted to a long crossbar extending the whole length of the fuselage and carrying at each end cranks for the elevator control wires which at intervals are carried through fibre guides socketted to the frame. The cranks of the elevators are concealed inside the rear end of the fuselage, whilst those of the rudder (which is fitted with duplicate cranks and wires) are external. A modified dual control is fitted, which allows the assistant pilot to work the elevator and rudder only. For this purpose a socket is mounted on the pivot bar into which can be inserted a plain steel tube which is normally carried in clips behind the pilot's back. A second rudder bar, the design of which is shown in Fig. 22, is carried under the dashboard and can readily be dropped into position into a square socket partially sunk into the floor of the cockpit and connected to the pilot's rudder bar by cranks and a link.

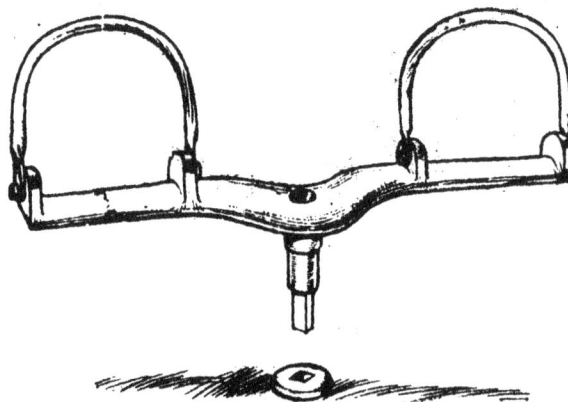

FIG. 22.

PERSONNEL.

Seats are provided for a crew of four, who are carried as follows:—

> One in the front cockpit.
> One in the pilot's seat.
> One at the pilot's side.
> One in the rear cockpit.

All can, if necessary, change places whilst the machine is in the air. Between the front cockpit and that of the pilot a sliding panel is provided through which the gunner can crawl. The seat at the side of the pilot folds up and slides back into a cavity under the coaming of the nacelle and when in this position allows access down a narrow and inclined passage-way to the rear cockpit. The machine can hardly have been designed to satisfy the requirements of the average pilot in regard to view, as from the pilot's seat it is very difficult to see the ground properly on account of the position of the lower main plane and the width of the fuselage.

ARMAMENT.

Two Parabellum guns are mounted, one in the front cockpit and one in the rear, and provision is made for mounting a third or for transferring one of the others on the floor of the rear cockpit, so that it can fire backwards and under the tail of the machine. For this purpose a large trap door, which is visible in the photograph B, is provided in the floor of the fuselage behind the rear cockpit. This trap door has celluloid windows and is normally kept closed by springs. It is lifted up by a small hand winch fitted with a ratchet. It is of passing interest to note that whereas in the Friedrichshafen a similar trap door was kept open by means of springs, in the A.E.G. springs are used to keep the door closed. In the front cockpit the gun is supported on a carriage which runs round a partially circular rail which is strongly supported from the fuselage by a framework of steel tubes. Forming part of this frame is an inclined steel tubular column, the base of which is fitted in a swivel bearing in the floor of the cockpit, and on this is mounted an adjustable seat for the gunner. A toothed rack runs round the rail and engages with a spur pinion driven by a hand wheel so that the gunner, when occupying his seat, swivels himself round as well as the gun. This gun mounting is shown in photograph C, and a diagrammatic section of the carriage is given in Fig. 23. The vertical swivel of the fork-ended gun carrier is locked by a ball-ended lever and a similar lever is employed for locking the carriage itself to its rail.

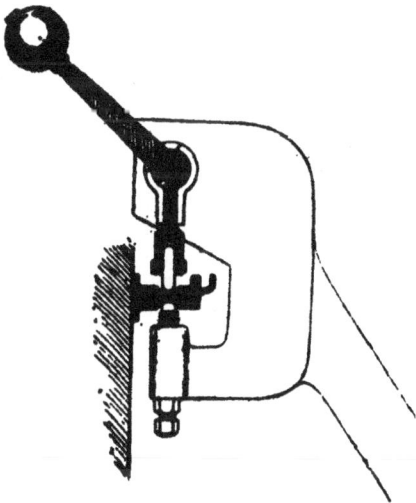

Fig. 23.

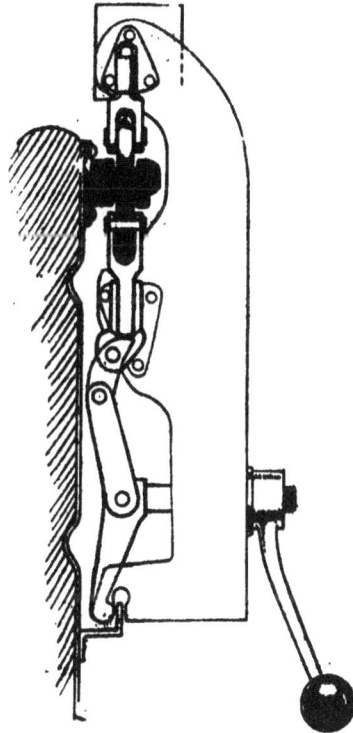

Fig. 24.

This action is accomplished by a cam device which depresses the roller of the carriage and squeezes the rail section between the roller and an adjustable set screw which normally just clears the groove on the under side of the rail. In order to prevent the forward gunner from shooting the tractor screws, preventative shields of light steel tube are carried between the upper edge of the forward cockpit and the inclined struts of the centre section. These impose a limit to the travel of the gun. In the rear cockpit the gun mounting is U shaped in plan form, and here again the principle of a carriage running on a rail and driven by a spur gear meshing with a toothed rack is employed, though in this case the gunner's seat does not revolve with the gun. The carriage is of a somewhat similar type to that used in the front cockpit, but the method of locking it is different. This is shown diagrammatically in Fig. 24. The rail is provided with grooves both above and below, there being two rollers at the top and one underneath

Normally, when the gun carriage is free, the latter is clear of the rail, but when the locking mechanism is brought into action it is forced upwards so that the rail is gripped between the rollers, thus avoiding any possibility of shake at this point, and at the same time a positive lock is obtained on a second rail carried below the first. When the ball-ended hand lever is tightened, its effect is to squeeze the lower rail between two jaws. The movable jaw is, however, connected up by a link to a small cam, the base of which abuts against the foot of a fork-ended rod which carries the lower roller and is free to move up and down in a guide, to the base of which the cam is pivotted. By this means a very secure and rapid locking device is obtained. In the front of the rear cockpit a locker is provided which would be capable of holding ammunition, and beneath this a series of racks of the type shown in Fig. 25. These racks are not strong enough to hold anything very heavy, and are placed approximately 5 inches apart. Their exact purpose is not known.

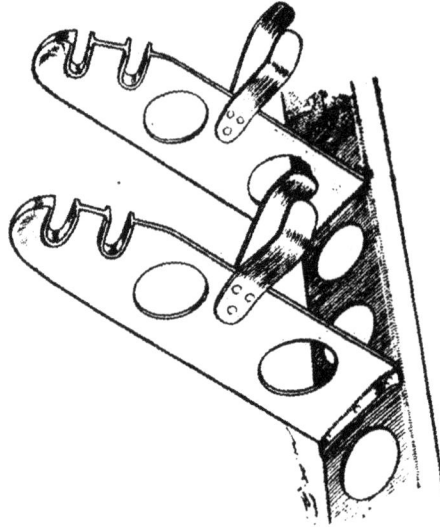

FIG. 25.

BOMBING GEAR

Three racks for holding twenty-five pounder bombs are installed on the machine; two side by side on the left side of the rear cockpit, and one on the right side of the petrol tanks in the space between the pilot's and rear cockpits. This rack is covered by a detachable wooden lid which acts as the floor of the narrow gangway mentioned above. Underneath the centre of the nacelle provision is made for carrying two or more large bomb racks, which, however, were not in use on this machine. Underneath the lower main plane, two at each side of the nacelle, are fixed bomb clips which are capable of supporting bombs roughly 8 inches in diameter. They are held in position by a belly-band consisting of two steel strips, clearly shown in the photograph B. Eleven-and-a-half inches in front of this clip is a bracket suitable for a circular section of 4 inches in diameter, and 13¼ inches in the rear of the clip is a second bracket suitable for a 5 inches diameter section. The bomb would thus appear to be 50 kgs. In the photograph the belly-bands are shown clipped out of the way. At their fixed end they are supported on a crosshead, a sketch of which is given in Fig. 26. This in turn is carried on a bracket clipped to a steel tube running parallel to the wing spars and braced thereto by tubular steel girders. The crosshead is free to swivel on the bracket against the action of a coiled spring which, when the bomb has been released, twists the crosshead round against a stop, so that the belly-band is forcibly swung round and now faces the direction of flight instead of lying edgewise on to it. The ends of the steel strips are swivelled on the crosshead, and here again coil springs are used, so that the tendency is for the belly-band to be held flat against the lower surface of the bottom main plane, and out of the way of the other clip.

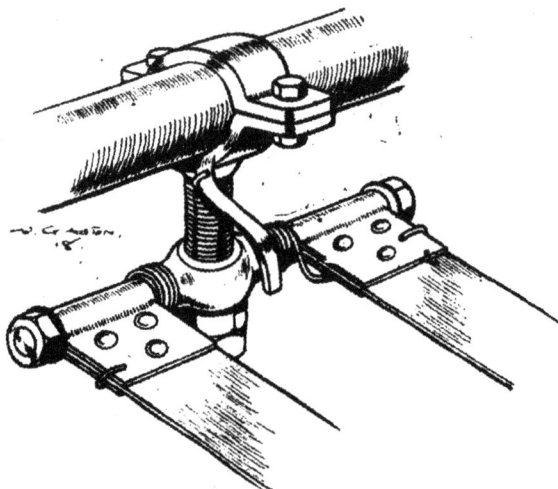

FIG. 26.

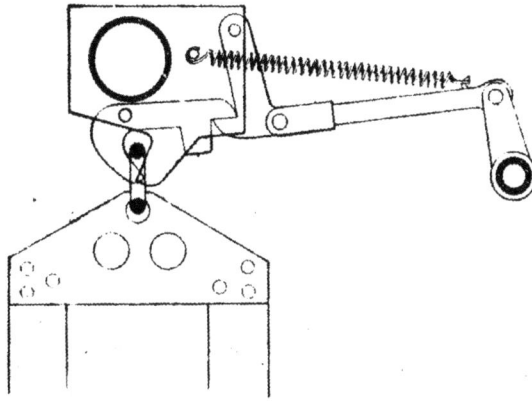

FIG. 27.

When the bombs are in position, the rings which are fitted on the free end of the belly-band are caught between the jaws of a trigger mechanism, illustrated diagrammatically in Fig. 27. This device is carried on the same tube which supports the crossheads, as already mentioned. Lying parallel to this tube and between it and the leading spar is a control rod fitted with two levers which are connected respectively to the two bomb trip gears, and this rod is operated by a quadrant lever mounted in the front cockpit. In order to allow one trip gear to be worked at a time, the link of the outer trip is provided with a slot where it is pivotted to the trigger release. On working the lever in the cockpit, therefore, its first action up to half way over the quadrant is to release the bomb nearest the nacelle, whilst a further movement releases the outer bomb. An exactly similar method is employed for operating the bombs carried underneath the other wing. The levers in the front cockpit are all mounted on a common bracket built up of steel tubes, and are arranged as follows:—First, there are the two levers which control the two bomb magazines in the rear cockpit. These are provided with thimbles and chains, so that they cannot be operated accidentally. Next, a single lever which controls the larger bomb clips on the right wing. These are capable of being secured by split pins inserted in their quadrants. Next, there is a lever which in this particular machine was furnished with no action at all, but is evidently designed for manipulating the large bomb carriers when these are installed. Behind it are, first, a single lever for the left hand outer bomb clips, and, finally, the lever for working the bomb magazine on the right hand side of the nacelle.

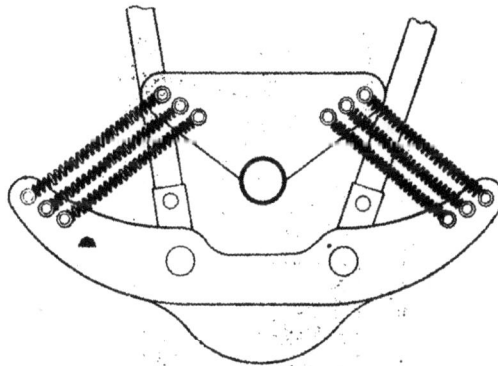

FIG. 28.

LANDING GEAR.

The landing gear of the A.E.G. bomber is simply an elaboration of that which has become practically a standard fitting on single and two-seaters, except that in this machine the gear is in duplicate. It consists of two axles carrying two wheels a-piece, and suspended from pairs of V struts. One pair is connected to the spars of the centre section immediately underneath the engine strut sockets, and the other to the spars midway between this point and the fuselage and at the same point from which diagonal struts are taken from the spars to the engine mounting and nacelle. This, together with the wire bracing of the landing gear struts provides a completely triangulated construction. The struts are, however, connected by ball joints similar to those used with the engine struts, so that in case of strain a certain amount of free movement can take place. The pairs of V struts carry at their foot a hollow steel crossbar having the section of a trough, and in this lies the axle which connects the two wheels. As shown in the sketch Fig. 28 and in the photograph D, the fixed beam has forward and rearward extensions, at each end of which are anchored the ends of the batteries of coil springs which act as shock absorbers, and at their other ends are hooked to a horn plate on the wheel axle. Each battery of springs, of which there are four to each axle, consists of ·18 springs. A yoke of stranded steel cable restricts the movement of the axle beyond a certain limit. The tyres are 32″×6″=810×150. A tail skid of massive proportions is used. This is of the shape shown in photograph E, and is built up entirely of welded steel. The springs against which it works are concealed inside the tail end of the fuselage.

WIRELESS.

The machine is internally wired for wireless, and a special dynamo for supplying current for this purpose and also for heating is installed on the right hand engine. This dynamo bears the following inscription :—

Telefunken.

J. P. Flieg: C 1916. Type D.
Alternating current 270 watts. 5 amperes. 600 frequency.
Continuous current 50 volts. 4 amperes. r.p.m. 4,500.

The dynamo is mounted on brackets acetylene-welded to the steel engine bearers, and is normally completely enclosed in a detachable fairing. Its position is clearly shown in photograph F. The dynamo drive embraces the pulley which is a standard fitting on the 260 H.P. Mercedes, but in this particular case the clutch gear whereby the driving pulley can be disconnected from the engine as required appears to have been discarded. Two sets of wires are taken from the dynamo inside flexible metal conduits to a pair of plugs situated at the junction of the fuselage and the right hand lower main plane. Here they terminate in plug sockets, so designed that the plugs cannot be inserted wrongly. One of these wiring circuits applies to the heating system, and wires for this purpose are carried to points in all three cockpits, whilst the other circuit is for wireless and terminates in a plug adapter in the rear cockpit. No wireless instruments were fitted. Two plug sockets for the heating installations are arranged in the rear cockpit; two in the pilot's cockpit and one for the forward gunner. A small plate on the pilot's dashboard carries the following inscription, but no definite information is given :—

F. T. Fitting.   W/T Set.
Aeroplanes.
Type 94.   NY   1125/16.
Fitting, No. 85a.
Driving propeller.   Type. Direct coupling.
Length of aerial wires. — — — —
Telefunken transmitter. — — — metres.
Huth transmitter. — — — — metres.
D transmitter. — — — metres.
G transmitter. — — — metres.

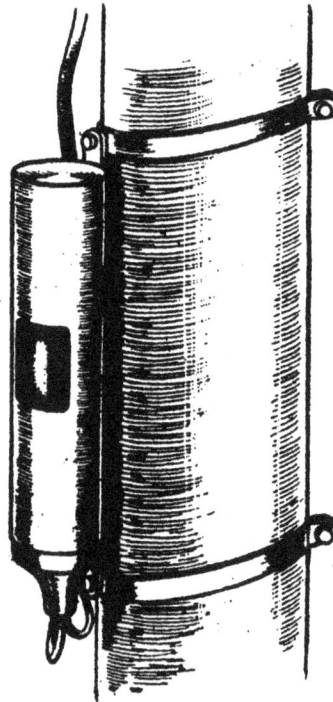

FIG. 29.

In addition to these two circuits, there is a lighting installation in conjunction with a battery carried in a box in the rear cockpit. From here, wires are taken to each cockpit and also to the tail and via the leading edge of the upper plane to the extreme outside strut of each wing. On these struts red and green lights are carried, the lamps for this purpose taking the form shown in Fig. 29. Inspection lights are provided at convenient points in each cockpit over the dashboard, instruments, etc.

For the most part the lighting wiring is contained inside a light celluloid conduit.

INSTRUMENTS.

These comprise twin engine revolution counters, twin air pressure gauges for the petrol supply, electric thermometer, altimeter, petrol level gauges, etc. All of these are of recognised types and call for no detailed description.

CAMOUFLAGE.

This machine is camouflaged in six different colours on a uniform system covering every portion. The colours are arranged in hexagons measuring roughly 18" across the flats, and the colours are sage green, reddish mauve, bluish mauve, black, blue and gray. These colours are not flat washes, but are softened by being stippled and splashed with paint of a lighter tone. The effect gained is well shown in photograph G. Considerable care appears to have been taken with this camouflage scheme, which is presumably effective.

FABRIC AND DOPE.

The fabric throughout is of good quality and the dope acetate of cellulose.

PROPELLER.

Diameter 10' 3.8"
± ·20".
Pitch 59.3".

The following table gives the thicknesses of the various laminæ used in construction of the air screw. The laminæ are numbered from the trailing to the leading edge.

No.	Material.	Thickness in inches.
1	Walnut	.73
2	Mahogany	.80
3	,,	.80
4	..	.80
5*	,.	.80
6	..	.80
7*	..	.40
8*	..	.40
9	,,	.80
10	Walnut	.83

* These laminations were of a quite different kind of mahogany, probably African.

Only one air screw has been seen and dimensioned. Thus it is unknown whether all air screws would have laminæ of similar thicknesses and of similar timbers. There is no apparent reason why these laminæ should be of different thicknesses. It is surmised that either the enemy is short of timber or that he has a highly scientific reason for so doing that we do not know. The port and starboard air screws rotate in opposite directions.

W. G. A.,

March, 1918.

J. G. WEIR,

Lieut.-Colonel,

Controller Technical Department.

A
INSTRUMENT BOARD IN PILOT'S COCKPIT.

B
UNDERSIDE OF THE NACELLE, SHOWING BOMB MAGAZINES AND RACKS,
ALSO TRAP DOOR IN REAR COCKPIT.

C

Front Cockpit and Gun Mount.

D

Undercarriage.

17

E
ARRANGEMENT OF TAIL.

F
THREE-QUARTER REAR VIEW OF FUSELAGE AND ENGINE MOUNTING.

18

MH. 3213

G
SIDE VIEW.

H
THREE-QUARTER FRONT VIEW. THE PROPELLER ON THE STARBOARD SIDE IS THE ORIGINAL; THAT
ON THE PORT A TEMPORARY SUBSTITUTE.

www.ingramcontent.com/pod-product-compliance
Lightning Source LLC
Chambersburg PA
CBHW081543090426
42741CB00014BA/3251